200 Ways to Balance Your Life

200 Ways to Balance Your Life

(Original title: *The Check Book: 200 Ways to Balance Your Life*)

BRET NICHOLAUS AND PAUL LOWRIE

BARNES
& NOBLE
BOOKS
NEW YORK

Originally published as
The Check Book: 200 Ways to Balance Your Life

This edition published by Barnes & Noble, Inc.,
by arrangement with New World Library

2001 Barnes & Noble Books

ISBN 0-7607-2510-1

Printed and bound in the United States of America

01 02 03 04 MC 5 4 3 2

FG

Acknowledgments

Bret: This book is dedicated to my loving wife, Christina, for being a source of constant joy in my life. They don't come any better! To my mom, Lorrie, and my late dad, Alan, for instilling in me so many of the thoughts and values contained in this collection. Finally, I wish to acknowledge the following members of my family just for being who they are: the late Raymond and Elsie Johnson, the late Herbert Nicholaus, Ruth Nicholaus, Violet Tjernberg, the late Ruth Janess, the late Melvin Carlson.

Paul: This book is dedicated to my mom, Janice, for reminding me to take the backroads of life, and my dad, Donald, for giving me a grasp on reality when my head is in the clouds; my sisters, Becky and Anita, for giving me other perspectives on life; my grandmother, Ruth Lowrie, for smiling so brightly every time I visit; and my surrogate grandparents, Willard and the late Eva Mallery, for providing my most memorable window to the past.

Matthew 25: 35–40

Introduction

A quick glance at the morning paper or the evening news will confirm a fact that is all too obvious to most of us: Our lives have become more and more stressful and, as a result, far less balanced. With ever-increasing responsibilities, households where both parents must work, and technological advancements like the Internet, we are left with less and less time for the simple, yet important, moments that life beckons us to embrace. The simpler times portrayed in such programs as *The Andy Griffith Show* seem long gone: an evening lemonade on the front porch, a real conversation around the dinner table, taking time to help someone less fortunate than ourselves. If only we could have a small taste of those times, or experience some sense of that balance in our own lives.

Welcome to *The Check Book!* You are about to uncover a collection of two hundred ideas and suggestions on how you can bring true balance back to your life and the lives of those around you. With a typical checkbook, you periodically sit down to balance your account; with *The Check Book* you are holding, you have a tool to help balance your life. Every suggestion you heed and accomplish will bring you one step closer to achieving that elusive balance — a balance that is sure to nourish your body, mind, and soul.

Each suggestion in this book falls into one of five "balance" categories:

- The suggestion brings **relaxation,** providing balance to a stressful day.
- The suggestion is the exact **opposite** of what you normally do, giving balance to your life by tipping the scale from one extreme to the other.
- The suggestion will bring you joy through its childlike **simplicity,** providing balance to an otherwise complicated, adult world.
- The suggestion involves performing an act of **kindness** for someone else, balancing our "me first" society.
- The suggestion offers **stability,** providing balance in an uncertain world.

You'll find that these five categories have been mixed together throughout the book. On one page you may find an idea that seems almost whimsical in its simplicity, yet a facing page may offer a suggestion profound enough to be life-changing. Some people may find every idea helpful; others may only need a handful of these suggestions to create the simplicity and balance each of us craves. Above each entry is an oval you can check if you'd like when you have completed the suggestion; in the back of the book are pages to write in your own suggestions, following the lead of the five categories above.

Whether your life consists of a growing number of daily meetings or you grow the grain that makes our daily bread, you can probably list dozens of ways your life has become unbalanced; from the city to the suburbs to the country, stress does not discriminate. While the easy, low-stress lifestyle may be a thing of the past, we each owe it to ourselves and those around us to strive for the simple life, the caring life — the balanced life — moment by moment.

So, just how balanced is your life? You're about to find out as you peruse the pages of *The Check Book!*

"The secret of life is balance, and the absence of balance is life's destruction."

— Hazrat Inayat Khan

"The key to everything is to find balance."

— George Lucas

Do something really special for someone, but challenge yourself to do it for a person who cannot pay you back; consider doing it anonymously. In the words of Ralph Waldo Emerson, "It is one of the most beautiful compensations of this life that no man can sincerely try to help another without helping himself."

Ask five people you know to write down on a piece of paper the one adjective that they think best describes you. Tell them to be honest. Collect all five pieces of paper. What do their perceptions tell you about yourself? Are you pleased with how you come across to others? Is there room for improvement?

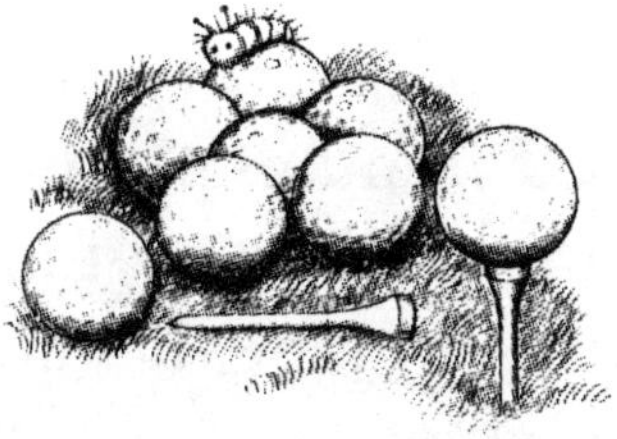

Whether you golf or not, go to a driving range and hit a bucket of golf balls. Begin by hitting everything as hard as you can; gradually decrease your power until near the end, you're barely swinging. Notice that as you decrease the power of your swing, your accuracy improves. There's a lesson about life here.

Spend thirty undisturbed minutes playing with a pet. Don't allow anything to interrupt this therapeutic time, not even the phone!

Start planning a vacation you've always wanted to take. Call a travel agency for brochures, talk to people who have been where you want to go, organize "planning sessions" with others who will go with you — make the preparation as much fun as the trip itself.

Spend an evening reminiscing with some old friends. Reflect on all the good times you've had together over the years.

Get a massage after a hard week of work.

Live one day as if it were your last day to live.

Take a good, long walk in the rain. Consciously try to feel it, hear it, and smell it like never before.

As you climb your own ladder of success, consciously reach down to bring others with you. Success is much sweeter and more meaningful when it's shared with others.

Do something out of the ordinary every night the week of your birthday. Don't limit your celebration of the big day to only twenty-four hours!

Take one hour to talk to an elderly person who's not a member of your family. Ask about his or her greatest experiences in life.

Make a list of your life's ten most wonderful moments and hang it on your refrigerator door.

The next time you're feeling depressed, do something to cheer someone else up. In the process, two people will feel better.

Attend a religious service every week for at least one full month. Don't let excuses stop you; commit to doing it and do it.

Throw away all your old socks and replace them with brand-new ones. Why do we spend $20,000 to replace a car every four years but hold onto a $5 pair of socks for seemingly twice as long?

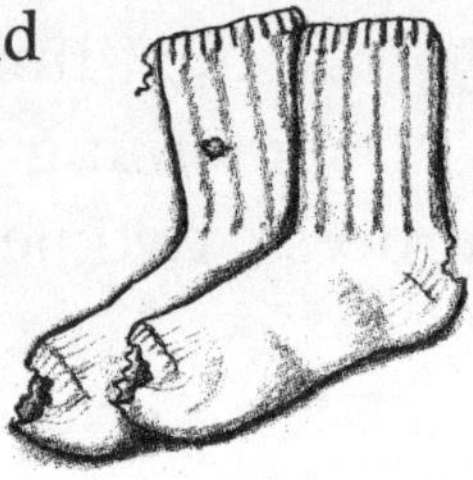

The very next time you're angry about something, release your frustration by engaging in a nondestructive activity: hit some tennis balls, lift weights, go running. . . . Put that negative energy to a positive use that benefits your body and mind.

Pay no attention to time for an entire weekend. Don't set your alarm clock. Cover all the clocks in your house. Don't wear a watch. Simply let things happen when they happen.

Take a two-hour walk at whatever pace feels comfortable for you. Although it sounds tiring, you may find it the most relaxing thing you've done in a long time.

Go an entire week without buying *anything* for yourself. (Don't forget to stock up on groceries!) Consider that for much of the world this is the norm, not the exception.

Get yourself a coloring book and a box of crayons and color a picture for someone you love.

"Raindrops on roses and whiskers on kittens . . ." Make a list of your ten favorite things, keep it in a convenient spot, and refer to it the very next time you feel sad.

Surprise your co-workers by bringing doughnuts, muffins, or bagels to work one day for no special reason. For something really unusual, provide snacks for another department, or for an outside business.

Find the most beautiful tree in your neighborhood and photograph it in each of the four seasons: budding in the spring, lush and green in the summer, turning colors in the fall, and snow- or ice-covered in the winter. Display the pictures of the changing seasons in a four-picture frame.

Play a Christmas CD or cassette on the Fourth of July, when Christmas is half a calendar away.

At Christmastime, six months before Independence Day, play a patriotic CD or tape.

When someone you know dies, write a brief letter to one of his or her survivors describing the impact — great or small — the person had on your life. They'll feel good reading it and you'll feel good writing it.

Go bowling with a group of friends. You'll have even more fun if you haven't bowled in ages.

Get into the habit of listening more and talking less. A person becomes wise by opening their ears, not their mouth.

Order stuffed French toast for breakfast. (Cherry and cream cheese stuffing is absolutely heavenly.)

Attend a children's choir concert. Even if they sing poorly, they'll sound great!

Finish a project well ahead of its deadline.

Take a picture the next time you're home and you find yourself saying, "What an incredible sunset!"

Make yourself a cup of hot chocolate, but fill the cup only halfway. Fill the entire upper half with rich whipped cream, letting it pile up above the rim. Top with chocolate sprinkles and savor every sip.

Give a portion of your Thanksgiving or Christmas Day leftovers to a poor family in your community. If possible, invite that family or individual to share the special day with you at your table.

Seek out and thank a war veteran. Rather than on Veteran's or Memorial Day, do it on an average day so it comes as a pleasant surprise.

For one full day, try to smile more than usual. Make it bigger and better than ever before. Since smiles are often contagious, you probably won't be the only one showing those pearly whites.

Do something really special to make a positive, lasting impact on a young child. Consider Jackie Robinson's epitaph: "A life is not important except in the impact it has on other lives."

Roast marshmallows over your outdoor grill. Add graham crackers and chocolate for great-tasting s'mores.

Try to develop a deeper trust and faith in God while relying less on your own abilities and perceived infallibilities. As Oliver Wendell Holmes Jr. said, "The great act of faith is when a man decides that he is not God."

Turn off the TV, radio, answering machine, lights — anything and everything that might distract you. Sit in a favorite location and do absolutely nothing for thirty minutes.

Expand your knowledge of the world. Sit down in front of a globe for thirty minutes and learn the geography and countries of a continent other than your own.

Enjoy a candlelight dinner in your home with someone special.

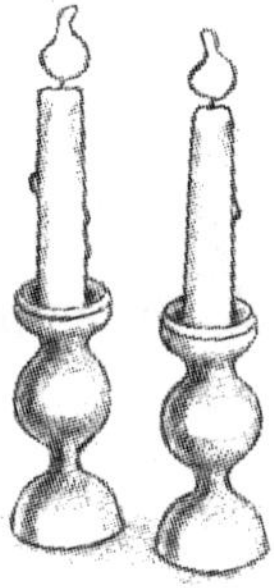

Welcome a new resident to your street by bringing them a small gift.

Go out on a limb and order something in a restaurant that you've never tasted before in your life.

Consciously increase your use of the phrases "I appreciate it" and "thanks a lot." Be grateful for even the smallest, most insignificant things others do for you.

Memorize a poem.

Buy a short nonfiction book about something in which you are not interested. Read it from cover to cover. Not only might your interest increase, it's a chance to broaden your horizons and open your mind.

Volunteer a couple of hours of your time for a good cause in your community or church.

Rent the nicest car you can afford for a three-day weekend getaway. Drive to a destination as far from home as time and energy allow — the key word here is *far*.

After a heavy rain, put on an old pair of boots and pants, go outside, and jump in the puddles.

Learn to say, "It's a pleasure to meet you" in five different languages. Use it whenever the opportunity arises, whether in a business or social setting. The people you meet will be honored that you have taken the time to learn something in their native tongue.

The next time you visit a crowded shopping mall, park as far as possible from the mall doors. It will keep you from getting stressed out as you drive around and around trying to find a spot up front. Equally important, the walk will do you good.

Enjoy a cold lemonade on a porch swing on a sultry summer night.

For one full weekend, turn off your answering machine. Experience the freedom of not having to get back in touch with anyone.

Start each morning with ten of the deepest and slowest breaths you can take. Perform this exercise before anything else.

Call someone you haven't talked to in at least five years and rekindle an old friendship. If you're asking yourself why they never call you anymore, chances are they're wondering why *you* never call *them!*

Get away from the city lights and take some time to look at the stars as they appear out in the country. Consider how small your problems really are as you ponder the expanse of the universe.

Tell someone something about yourself that you've never told anyone before.

Take a thirty-minute bubble bath. Get the water temperature just right, go heavy on the bubbles, and lose yourself in the cloud of foam.

Test-drive an expensive high-performance automobile that you couldn't afford to actually buy.

Stop praying for things and start praying for people.

Double your ability level at something. If, for example, you feel you can't sing, take a few voice lessons; stick with it and you could become an accomplished singer.

Make an annual budget for yourself. Create a balance sheet of your projected income and expenses for the next twelve months, including everything you can think of, from auto insurance to grocery bills to entertainment expenses.

Rake up a huge pile of leaves and spend some time jumping into it.

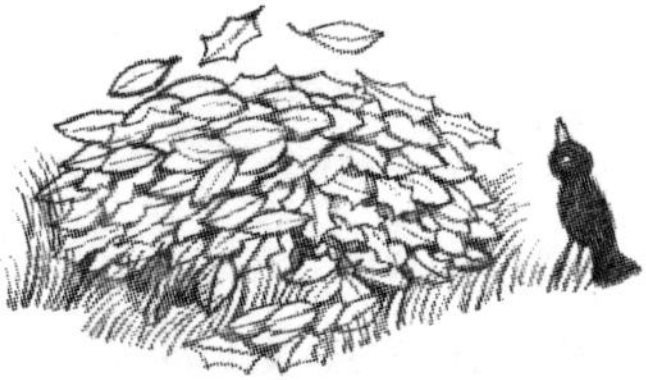

Buy an autograph book and ask ordinary people to sign it. For example, collect the signature of a commercial airplane pilot, of someone who's been to the top of the Eiffel Tower, of someone who shook hands with a U.S. president. . . . Below each name, cite their achievement. The people you ask to sign will be thrilled!

Avoid snapping back the next time you're in a conversation and someone states an opinion that differs radically from your own. Don't give them the pleasure of engaging you in an argument. If you don't answer back, the discussion will shift to another topic.

Lie down in a field or park on a lazy summer day and spend some time simply watching the clouds roll by.

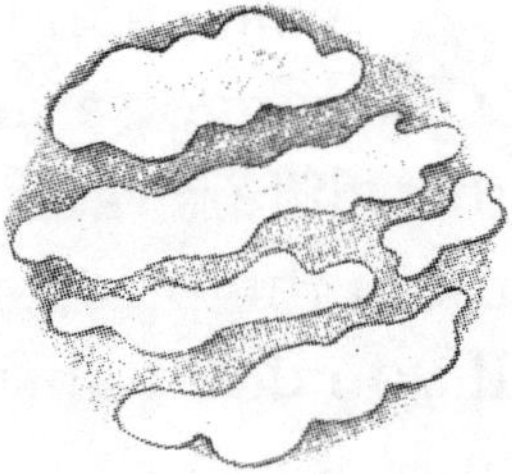

Give $50 to a family you know is struggling to make ends meet. Give the money to a family you hardly know rather than one you know well.

Do something for free that you would normally expect to be paid for.

Stop talking about writing that book you've always wanted to write and start writing it. Dedicate yourself to completing just two pages a week. By the end of the year you'll have written a 100-page book!

Show extreme humility the next time you win and extreme dignity the next time you lose. Boastful winners and sore losers — in a sport, on the job, or in life — are rarely respected by anyone.

Leave your Christmas tree up until the middle of January. After a hectic Christmas and New Year's, you'll actually have time to truly enjoy it.

Plan a "progressive dinner" with some friends. Have the soup or salad course at one house, the main course at a second home, and the dessert at a third. It's the equivalent of three parties in one night, and a lot of fun.

Spend one full hour watching a televised sporting event you've never had any interest in. You'll surely gain some knowledge about the sport, and you just might walk away feeling excited about it.

Find a hero for yourself. We all need someone to inspire and motivate us to a higher level.

Have a party at your home where the evening's entertainment is a sing-along of well-known tunes from yesteryear. A little nostalgia feels pretty good sometimes.

Sit on a quiet sea- or lakeshore and watch the summer sun set over the water.

Memorize a really funny — but clean — joke and tell it to at least five people during the week.

Attend a church or temple of a different denomination or religion than your own. Enter the service with an open mind and an open heart.

Get in your car (where you'll be safe), drive to an open field or lakeshore, and watch a lightning storm in all its wonder.

For one month, consult a dictionary and learn one new and difficult word each day. By the end, you'll know thirty new words to enrich your conversations.

Connect the lawn sprinkler on a hot summer day and run through the water. Remember how enjoyable it was as a child? It still is!

Hang some wind chimes in a location where you can hear them every time a breeze blows by.

Learn to whistle a favorite tune as well as you possibly can. (Have you ever noticed that people who whistle generally are happy and care-free?)

Get down on the floor and allow a tail-wagging dog to lick your face. Let go of any inhibitions you might have.

Get out of your local news "box" and read the paper from a city far away from your own. If, for example, you live in Los Angeles, pick up an Atlanta paper; if you live in Atlanta, read a daily newspaper from the West Coast. This is one of the easiest ways to discover different slices of life.

Say "I love you" to someone who has rarely, or never, heard you say those words.

Plant something in your yard in memory of someone who has passed away. It will serve as a constant reminder of that person's life.

Complete all your Christmas shopping before Thanksgiving. Allow yourself to enjoy the season without the pressure of huge crowds, long lines, and parking nightmares.

Contact that person you've been saying you're going to get together with for the last year or two and set a date.

Have someone tickle you until it drives you crazy.

Eat something you've always disliked and haven't tasted in at least three years. Be willing to give it another chance, as opinions change over time.

Conquer one fear you've always had — even if it's just a small one. As John Wayne said, "Courage is being scared to death and saddling up anyway."

Beautify your home in the spring with colorful azalea plants.

The next time you receive exceptional service in a mediocre restaurant, leave a 30 percent tip. It's only 15 percent more than customary, but it will mean a lot more than that to your server.

Buy a roll of film and take pictures of things you would normally never think of photographing. After the pictures are developed, choose the most unusual one and have it framed.

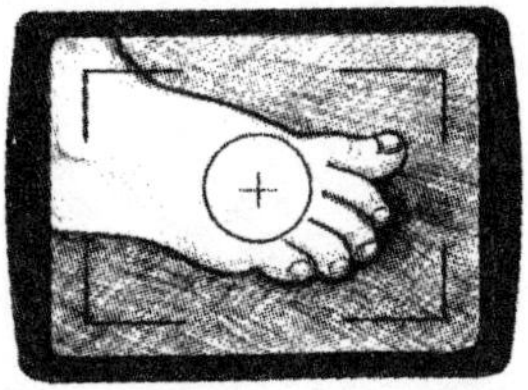

Start a brand-new friendship with someone.

Wake up early enough to do something before you go to work that you typically do after you get home.

Strive to find something good in everything. Remember that a beautiful rose often grows at the end of a thorny stem.

Do something sweet for your mother, father, or both that you've never, ever done before.

Offer to do the weekly grocery shopping for an older or ill person who has a hard time getting out of the house. Refuse any tip he or she might offer.

Write down your three most negative traits on an index card. Periodically refer back to the list and do everything in your power to correct them.

Read (or re-read) one of the four Gospels of the Bible — Matthew, Mark, Luke, or John — all the way through. Cover one chapter a night until you're done.

Get a group of friends or family members together and spend an afternoon at an orchard or farm picking your own fruit.

Be willing to accept your limitations in life; each of us requires the skills and knowledge of others to be successful. Rome wasn't built in a day, but more importantly, it wasn't built by just one person.

Sincerely ask someone you've wronged to forgive you.

Take a late autumn walk when the aroma of burning wood fills the crisp air.

Stop and offer to help someone who's having roadside problems.

Enhance the wonderful feeling of anticipation for a big event by literally crossing the days off your calendar.

Cut down your own Christmas tree.

Bake a batch of homemade cookies and leave them with a note on a friend's doorstep.

Offer to host a sleepover for the children of some parents you know well. The children and you will have a lot of fun, and you'll give their mom and dad a much-needed break.

Write a heartfelt song or poem about someone or something you love. Allow your passion to flow.

Buy yourself an indoor fountain (small ones are available for around $50). The peaceful sound of the bubbling, cascading water is sure to relax you after a busy day.

For at least one week, take fifteen minutes a day to sit in a chair and do nothing but think about relaxing things. Don't think about anything even remotely stressful; let every thought soothe your mind, body, and soul.

Write a one-sentence mission statement for your life and carry it around with you.

For one full week, completely deny yourself one thing you typically crave every day: your favorite food, TV show, music. . . . Don't cheat!

Buy yourself a good recording of Handel's *Messiah*. Written in just twenty-four days, it's one of the greatest and most beautiful musical compositions of all time.

Squeeze some oranges or grapefruits by hand on an old-fashioned juicer and drink in one of the simple pleasures of days gone by.

Take "baby steps" to start that overwhelming project you've been putting off. Don't panic yourself by looking at what it takes to get from A to Z; do what you must to get from A to B, and then from B to C, C to D, and so on. Use "baby steps" in everything you do and you'll eliminate a lot of stress.

Discover and claim a secret place that's all your own.

Buy a coffee-table book of New England in autumn. Page through its pictures whenever you feel stressed out.

Eat breakfast for dinner. No rule states that eggs, sausage, and pancakes can't be enjoyed as much at 6 A.M. as at 6 P.M.

Share with a special person a flaming dessert that's prepared tableside.

Sit down and write three jokes about yourself. If you can take yourself lightly, you won't be so defensive when others allude to your flaws and foibles.

Go an entire day without saying one negative comment about anything or anyone! To really test your resolve, pick a day when you're going to be talking to a lot of people — at a party, for example.

Wear a humorous tie with your most solemn business suit, or a flamboyant pair of earrings with your most sophisticated outfit.

Have a fun-filled pillow fight in bed with your significant other.

In all aspects of life, learn to be tough on yourself but go easy on others. Set extremely high standards and values for yourself, but be slow to judge others who don't reach them.

Choose a week to get a minimum of fifty-six hours of sleep over the course of seven nights. Take this charge seriously and, at least for that week, you'll feel like a new person.

Celebrate "Rose Week." Each day of the week, give a single rose to someone in your life who deserves special recognition. (A small box of chocolates can serve as a great substitute for a rose.)

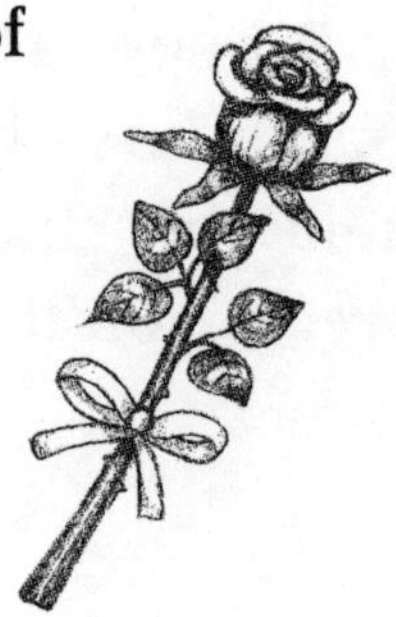

Spend one full day paying careful attention to all the objects around you that you typically take for granted. Find the beauty in details you usually overlook: the fine wood grain on a table, the fizzing in a carbonated beverage, a piece of popped corn, a honeybee on a clover. . . .

Make a serious and diligent effort to eliminate one bad habit in your life.

Immerse yourself in the peaceful sound of a babbling brook.

Take a horse-drawn carriage or sleigh ride.

Join a club or organization that interests you and take an active role in it right from the start.

Learn to identify the chirps and warbles of at least five different species of birds in your area.

Go for a Sunday afternoon drive with no destination in mind. Just drive until something catches your eye.

Write your own obituary while you're alive and well. Be honest with yourself as you write it: Have you been the type of person that people will truly miss someday? If not, make some changes in your life to reflect how you really want people to feel about you once you're gone.

Memorize and begin to live your life by this quote from Henry David Thoreau: "I make myself rich by making my wants few."

Offer a piece of potentially life-changing advice to someone you know and care about. Offer it; don't force it.

Pick a bunch of wildflowers from a field or forest to brighten a room in your home.

Do something to your hair that you've never done before. Change your style, color, length, part — anything — but change something.

The next time someone gives you well-deserved recognition in front of a group, defer all the credit to others. Put your ego last.

Try to find someone who's a true fan of both Elvis Presley and Bach. There's a lesson to be learned from this person.

Attend a small town's historical celebration or re-enactment.

Devote yourself to overcoming one seemingly insurmountable obstacle in your life. Remember: People don't fail, they quit.

Ask yourself this question: What is my worst enemy in life? (Examples: distrust of others, lack of self-esteem, too much time away from my family. . . .) Commit yourself to destroying this foe.

Get away from the computer and play a game the old-fashioned way: with boards, cards, dice, or spinners. Pick a board game you haven't played in years, invite some friends over, and make a night of it.

Dressing appropriately, take a thirty-minute walk outdoors on the coldest day of the year. Take deep, cleansing breaths of the crisp, cold air as you move along.

Become a sponge soaking in even the smallest of life's moments. Allow yourself to be overwhelmed by the simplest pleasures the world has to offer.

Give someone a cash tip who normally doesn't receive tips. Of course, do it only to reward exceptional service.

Start a scrapbook of your life's highlights from this year forward. Include everything from tickets for sporting events or concerts you attend to postcards or photos of places you visit.

Say something to make at least three people really happy in one day.

Pack a picnic for two and enjoy it in the most scenic location you know.

Take a bad situation and try to make something good come out of it. Remember, when you come to a dead-end street, you can always turn around.

Learn to take a "whatever" attitude when things don't go exactly as planned. There are too many major issues in this world that need solving to let small problems upset you. After all, as the late columnist Sydney J. Harris said, "If a little thing has the power to make you angry, does that not indicate something about your size?"

Turn a Friday or Saturday night into a mini film festival. Call up some friends, rent three of your all-time favorite films, get comfortable, and start watching. If you begin around 6 P.M., you'll get through all of them by about midnight.

The next time you're in a group discussion, take the side in an argument that you would normally argue against. Fight as passionately on this side of the fence as you would on the other. It will be difficult, but you will learn a lot from this exercise.

Commit yourself to eliminating one prejudice you have. Make sure your actions reflect your new attitude.

Put a bird feeder or bath in your yard where you can easily view its daily visitors.

Change something about your demeanor that will make others feel more comfortable around you.

Choose a weekend to forget about grams of fat and calories. Eat anything and everything you crave. People need an occasional break from careful, controlled eating just as much as they need a break from their job.

Write yourself an IOU that comes due in six months and put it in an envelope. Write down whatever you feel you owe yourself: A vacation? A new TV? A healthier body? Remember that you now owe it to yourself to accomplish or fulfill whatever you've written on that piece of paper. Don't default!

Stop and buy something a young child is selling even if you don't need it. (Don't wish them "good luck" without purchasing their product.) Consider tipping them as well. After you've paid, leave them with some encouraging words.

Start a daily journal in which you record at least one simple joy or blessing you experience each day.

Skip rocks on a lake or pond.

Try something you once vowed you would never be willing to do. (Parachuting, anyone?)

Celebrate a "Slow Down Day." Do everything at a decelerated pace: speak slower, drive slower, walk slower — even think slower.

Reread a favorite book from your childhood. Don't overlook the moral or lesson of the story; it's probably as applicable to you as an adult as when you were a child.

Buy a package of yellow smiley-face stickers and put one on the back of every envelope you mail. Use them especially when paying bills that drain your checking account.

Place one truly unique or inspiring object in every room of your home, including the bathroom. In other words, have something meaningful in each room that you can share with others.

Ponder the awesome breadth of history. Within its vast picture, consider how different your life would have been if you had lived 100, 200, or even 1,000 years ago.

Celebrate your half-birthday, exactly six months after your real birthday. Buy a cake, go out for dinner, or have a party — just be sure to celebrate it one way or another.

Ask yourself, "Where will I be in ten years if I continue doing what I'm doing now?" If you don't like the answer, it's up to you to take action. Life is a two-lane road on which you're either moving toward or running from something.

Laugh so hard that you cry.

Throw a surprise party for someone.

On a sunny winter day, find a bright, warm spot indoors where the sun's rays shine through the window. Sit in the sun with your eyes shut and simply enjoy the warmth.

Roll down all of your car windows, making your car a virtual convertible. Take to the open road and turn up your favorite music. Let the wind and songs surround you and lift your spirits.

Go to a playground — not to sit and watch others but to enjoy the equipment yourself.

Turn over a large rock or log and take a few minutes to carefully observe the activity going on in the grass or soil below. Don't forget to put it back when you're done.

Learn to say "please" for even the smallest, most simple requests.

Buy a bottle of bubbles with a wand — not for your or others' children but for yourself.

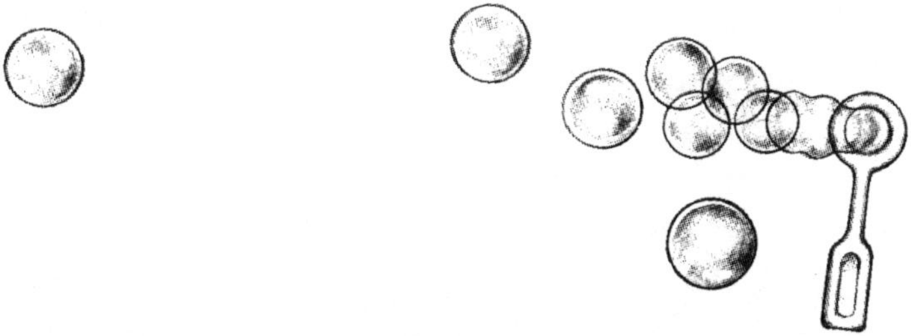

Get yourself to the top of something: the rooftop of your house, the top floor of a large building, the top of a hill. . . . Pause for a few minutes and experience the liberation of being removed from the busyness below.

Take a route to work that's completely different from your usual commute. You'll probably discover places you never expected just beyond your usual path and you'll break the monotonous pattern.

Allow yourself to become mesmerized by something natural — like ripples on water or a soaring bird.

Rent a favorite movie from your childhood — one you haven't seen in a long time — and try to watch it with the same enthusiasm you had as a youngster.

Buy yourself a toy that would make the typical ten-year-old green with envy. Once you've bought it, take pleasure in using it. It really is okay not to act your age sometimes.

Thoroughly clean something that's needed it for a long, long time: your car, your dresser drawers, your filing cabinet, your gutters. . . .

Abstain from drinking any alcohol the next time you attend a party.

The next time you *host* a party at your house, refrain from serving alcohol of any kind. (Who wrote the rules, anyway?) Instead, create for your guests some unusual and delicious nonalcoholic specialty drinks.

Contact your travel agent and request promotional material for both Alaska and Hawaii — two of our most beautiful and awe-inspiring states. Hang some of the best pictures of each in your office or recreation room.

Allow yourself to cry about something you've been wanting to cry about for a long time.

Begin a new hobby that doesn't require too much work to enjoy.

Spend a weekend in a quaint little town. Soak in the atmosphere and live the small-town lifestyle for a couple of days.

Learn to let others "have the stage." In your conversations, be extra careful not to one-up someone else's stories or statements. If someone tells you about their wonderful five-day family trip to Florida, don't immediately follow it with the story of your two-week cruise in the Caribbean.

Buy something for yourself that you can't really afford but that you also can't afford to go without. In other words, make a purchase that will make your life easier, more productive, or less stressful — thus paying significant "dividends" in the long run.

Take some kids to the zoo for an afternoon.

Is there one thing that you've always said you were going to do but have never done? *Do it soon!*

We Invite You to Write Your Own Suggestions . . .

Write two suggestions that bring you **relaxation**, providing balance to a stressful day.

•

•

Write two suggestions that are the exact **opposite** of what you normally do, giving balance to your life by tipping the scale from one extreme to the other.

Write two suggestions that bring you joy through their childlike **simplicity**, providing balance to an otherwise complicated, adult world.

Write two suggestions involving performing acts of **kindness**, balancing our "me first" society.

Write two suggestions that give your life **stability**, providing balance in an uncertain world.

About the Authors

Bret Nicholaus, 30, and **Paul Lowrie**, 31, are full-time writers. Together, they have written nine books, including the bestselling *The Conversation Piece*. They are also the creators of two board games, a page-a-day calendar, and a syndicated radio show. Graduates of Bethel College in St. Paul, Minnesota, their first book was inspired by their experiences in college. Now with nearly half a million books in print, their often hectic schedules as authors inspired them to write *The Check Book*. Through this project, they hope to help others simplify their lives in ways that each of them has found helpful and rewarding. Bret lives with his wife in the Chicago area. Paul lives in Yankton, South Dakota.